WHAT NOT TO DO AT SSB INTERVIEWS

LET'S ENSURE YOU DON'T GET REJECTED

GOURAV VIVEK KULKARNI

Copyright © Gourav Vivek Kulkarni
All Rights Reserved.

ISBN 978-1-68563-862-7

This book has been published with all efforts taken to make the material error-free after the consent of the author. However, the author and the publisher do not assume and hereby disclaim any liability to any party for any loss, damage, or disruption caused by errors or omissions, whether such errors or omissions result from negligence, accident, or any other cause.

While every effort has been made to avoid any mistake or omission, this publication is being sold on the condition and understanding that neither the author nor the publishers or printers would be liable in any manner to any person by reason of any mistake or omission in this publication or for any action taken or omitted to be taken or advice rendered or accepted on the basis of this work. For any defect in printing or binding the publishers will be liable only to replace the defective copy by another copy of this work then available.

To All Defence Aspirants..

Contents

Preface   *vii*

Acknowledgements   *ix*

1. Chapter 1   1
2. Selecting The Date For Ssb Interview   8
3. Documentation For The Ssb Interview   10
4. Traveling From Home For The Ssb Interview   12
5. Reporting For The Ssb Interview   16
6. What Not To Do On Day 1: Documentation And Screening Tests   18
7. What Not To Do On Day 2: Psychological Tests And Personal Interview   28
8. What Not To Do On Day 3: Group Tasks Day 1   36
9. What Not To Do On Day 4: Group Tasks Day 2   43
10. What Not To Do On Day 5: The Board Conference   46
11. Traveling Back Home From The Ssb Interview   48

Preface

A career in the Armed Forces is the most satisfying and promising way of life. One gets the best of adventure activities and can sumptuously satisfy their craving for a life of respect, discipline, honour and what not!

It is true that Officers are not born but are shaped out of talented youth who have those Officer Like Qualities. To become an officer in the Army, Navy or Air Force, it is mandatory that the candidate undergoes testing at respective Services Selection Board.

A Services Selection Board Interview (referred as SSB Interview hereafter) is not a mundane table-chair interview but is full of a wide range of tasks and spans over a period of 5 days. There is a plethora of material available at various sources that would rightly guide the candidate to crack the SSB Interview but there are limited resources that could guide candidates from a candidate's perspective as to "What not to do at SSB Interviews".

This book intends to precisely aim at that area. The contents and cost has been kept short and crisp so that this book can reach out to all those worthy aspirants looking for a career in the Armed Forces with the intent of service to the nation.

The contents of this book are a result of my experiences at a total of 22 SSB Interviews that I had appeared from the first one as a fresher in February 2017 to the last one as a repeater in January 2021. I was not recommended in any of them so I would not be eligible to guide for recommendation but I would surely be the most eligible author to pen down some suggestions as to what should be avoided at SSB Interviews to ensure recommendation.

This book is a result of self introspection of failures which in my opinion is as important as a success story!

I'm sure these experiences will make you aware of what not to do at SSB Interviews to get recommended and fulfill the dream of wearing the Uniform!

Jai Hind!
Gourav Vivek Kulkarni
Belgaum, Karnataka, India
March 2021

Acknowledgements

Sincere thanks to my parents, Adv. Vivek G Kulkarni and Roopa Kulkarni for their unconditional moral support and motivation during all the attempts. This would have not been possible without their words of courage and motivation to win after every failure. That was the sole thing that kept me going.

Special words of thanks to a few close friends mentioned as below for being a part of this journey and for never letting my morale go down!

Sincere thanks to you all!

Pratik Deshpande
Akshay Takalkar
Ranjit Desai
Abhishek Basapuri
Avinash Biradar
Amit Hande
Gaurang Kulkarni
Guruprasad Karlekar
Rohan Kuduchkar
R Dinesh Kumar
Kalyani Kulkarni
Priyanka Deo
Priyanka Koli-Bilachi
Divya Lagmavar

CHAPTER ONE

In order to join the Army, Navy or the Air Force, it is imperative that for most of entries, a qualifying examination has to be passed. With the advent of advanced technologies, these exams for the Navy and Air Force are being taken online and are called INET and AFCAT respectively.

It is necessary that the candidate is clear with the service that he/she wants to join. This is a complete matter of choice and there cannot be any comparison between the three arms as all are equally capable of combat in their own roles. There may be a few candidates who wish to join the Armed Forces for the Uniform, some for discipline while some for sports and adventures. Thus is a matter of personal choice. However, it is imperative that this choice is made well in advance so that the same can be indicated in the online application.

Whether it is the Written Examination or Online examination, the syllabus is more or less the same with an exception being the NDA and NA Examination in which 12^{th}Class CBSE Mathematics is a mandatory paper. In all other examinations, Mathematics is of matriculation level and any candidate can clear it without any kind of special preparation.

While preparing for the Examination:

- Don't buy too many books as you are more likely to be overwhelmed with the subject matter covered to different levels of comprehension in different books. Best is to stick to one book that covers the entire syllabus
- Don't ignore test series and practice sets or old question papers as they can be the best guide as to what can appear
- Don't leave any section of the syllabus, rather study the trend of questions and prepare every bit of it to the necessary extent
- In subjects related to Science and Technology, do read certain current advancements in respective fields in addition to the theoretical concepts
- Don't be afraid, you can do it!

The preparation of examination is more or less a continuous process looking at the varied schedule of various examinations during the year for the three services. It is necessary that the candidate keeps an eye on the advertisements in Employment News or on the websites for the notifications of applications. Once the advertisement is out, it is required that the application process should be started.

During the application process:

- Don't wait for the last day to rise and complete the application on the day of opening or latest within the next two or three days. Examination cities have certain ceiling on number of candidates and may get full
- Don't enter any kind of false information as it may make or break your dreams in near future. Thus being honest in declaring any information is a must

- Once the application is completed, save a PDF of the same in a designated folder. This may be required while reporting for the SSB Interview if mentioned in the instructions
- Don't mess up the choice or preference of services because if you become eligible for multiple academies, you will be called for the interview as per your most preferred and eligible service only
- Don't make any mistakes in entering the details of payment done as it may make your name appear in the fictitious payments' list

Once the application is done with, it is required that the candidate regularly checks his/her email or the concerned website for the Admit Cards. Admit Cards for AFCAT may be sent by email while for other exams, the candidate needs to download it from the website.

The Admit Card needs to be preserved for future reference as it is mandatory to carry the same to the SSB Interview. In the following sections, certain tips for written and online exams have been elaborated.

1.1 Written Examination

As on date, two examinations are conducted in written mode viz. the National Defence Academy & Naval Academy (NDA & NA) Examination and the Combined Defence Services Examination (CDSE). The candidate needs to report at the designated centre in the set of cities notified and chosen by the candidate. Having appeared for both of them multiple times, I am eligible to give you certain valuable insights.

1.1.1 Conduct

The candidate has to travel to the city where the examination venue is selected at their own cost as there is no travel allowance given for the written exam. It is necessary to locate the examination centre well in advance to avoid last minute rush. The candidates are issued with the question papers as per their series A, B, C or D. The corresponding Optical Mark Reader (OMR) Sheet has to be filled accurately and exam shall be commenced when told to do so.

The duration of examination varies as per the paper and subject. Hence it is required that the candidate is physically ready for the same. Once the time is up, the OMR sheet has to be handed over to the invigilator and the candidate can take the question paper along with them.

Some points to remember:

- Choose a city that is nearest to your place of residence to avoid any last minute hurry
- Report at the examination centre at least 30 minutes prior to the reporting time mentioned in the Admit Card. Never be late since this is the first step towards building discipline to join the Armed Forces
- Although nobody is there is judge your behavior, it is imperative that from this stage itself a disciplined approach is undertaken

1.1.2 How to score more

This is the most asked question when the outputs of the exam are thought of. Since this is a written test whose responses have to be marked on an OMR sheet, extra care needs to be taken by the candidate.

I would like to tell a hack with which, a candidate can probably score a few extra marks. This was told to us in 2013 by one of my professors, Prof. Udaysingh Rajput when I was preparing for the NDA and NA Examination. It goes as follows.

Out of all the questions, there are a few questions in which you are confused between two options only and you are quite sure that one of them is correct. If the negative marking is $1/3^{rd}$, choose only three such questions and if the negative marking is $1/4^{th}$, choose only four such questions. But make sure all the other answers marked by you are correct and not guessed.

Out of whatever number of questions chosen by you, in the worst case, answers to all of them may be wrong. In that case, you will be losing marks for only one correct answer. But the probability of this is very low. If one answer is correct and remaining are wrong, the candidate can score bonus marks which would have otherwise not been scored. In the best case, if all the answers guessed are correct, the candidate can get those many bonus marks which he/she would have never got. In this manner, the candidate can score some bonus marks and strengthen the chances of clearing the written examination.

Some points to remember:

- Don't mark the answer you are completely sure of it as mistakes cannot be undone on OMR Sheets
- Don't guess any answer however bold the guess may be because it can hamper the overall score if wrong
- Don't make any mistakes in marking the right answer against the right question number

1.1.3 A few things to refrain from

- Don't skip breakfast at any cost since the examinations are conducted in quick succession and the time gap in between may be insufficient to have something
- Don't be late at any cost
- Don't make any mistakes while filling up the OMR Sheet especially with the Roll number, as it may lead to cancellation of candidature
- Don't do anything other than that mentioned in the instructions
- Don't carry anything other than a pen, Admit card and identity proof to the examination hall

1.2 Online Examination

As on date, the Indian Navy Entrance Test (INET) and Air Force Common Admission Test (AFCAT) are conducted in online mode at the designated computer centers in the cities notified and chosen by the candidate. Having appeared for both of them multiple times, I am eligible to give you certain valuable insights.

1.2.1 Conduct

The only variation between this exam and the written exam is the mode of conducting the exam. Unlike the OMR sheets that need to be marked in case of the Written Exam, in this, the option has to be selected and marked on the computer display.

The candidates are checked for possession of any prohibited items and are allotted to designated computer labs. The candidates are allowed to log in before a certain time corresponding to the start of the examination. The instructions have to be read carefully and the method of marking the correct answers has to be clearly understood. Once the examination begins, the automatic clock shall keep the time and indicate it accordingly. The paper is automatically submitted once the time is up.

As in case of the INET, there is only one test while in case of the AFCAT, there is an additional test called Engineering Knowledge Test (EKT) required for commission into the Technical Branch of the Indian Air Force. The method of conducting the EKT is same as that of the AFCAT.

1.2.2 How to score more

The tips mentioned for the written test are very much applicable in this case as well. However, there is a hidden advantage of these online tests. It is that the candidate can amend or cancel the option marked at any point of time. This can definitely save a number of marks of the candidate in event of marking of the wrong option.

1.2.3 A few things to refrain from

- In this case too, don't skip breakfast as the examination sessions are controlled by online servers and any kind of glitch can result into delays
- Don't be late at any cost
- Don't divert from the instructions
- Don't carry anything other than a pen, Admit card and identity proof to the examination hall. Rough sheets shall be provided at the lab
- Avoid guessing the answer as this last minute rush can cost you marks

CHAPTER TWO

Selecting the Date for SSB Interview

After completion of the written or online examinations, the result is announced on the respective website or communicated via email. This is the point where most of the candidates are quite confused and apprehensive if appearing for the first time. I have even seen the same level of apprehension in repeaters as well because after all, the aim is to get recommended.

For the Indian Army, there are two entries, one with a written exam (NDA, IMA, OTA) and one without on the basis of performance in graduation (TGC, SSC(Tech), NCC etc). The facility to select a convenient date is applicable generally for all the entries except the NDA and CDSE. But if required, the candidate may be given an option to choose a convenient date for these entries too. However, the Selection Centre is allotted by them and no change in the same is permitted. On logging in, the candidate can see a number of dates of available batches. The most convenient one may be selected. There are four Selection Centres viz. Selection Centre North at Kapurthala in Punjab, Selection Centre East at Prayagraj in Uttar Pradesh, Selection Centre Central at Bhopal in Madhya Pradesh and

Selection Centre South at Bangalore in Karnataka. Each of these selection centres has multiple boards for selection to the Indian Army and is called Service Selection Boards. Bhopal and Bangalore have one board each for selection to the Indian Navy as well.

For the Indian Navy, if it is an NDA or NA or CDSE entry, generally the date and venue is allotted by the authorities. If the allotted date isn't convenient, there is always an option to avail the absentee batch. But a word of advice would be to avoid absentee batches as the number of candidates will be large. For the INET entry to various branches of the Indian Navy, there is a provision to choose a convenient date. Apart from the boards at Selection Centre Central and Selection Centre South, there are three more Naval Selection Boards located at Coimbatore in Tamil Nadu, Visakhapatnam in Andhra Pradesh and Kolkata in West Bengal.

For the Air Force, the candidate has a greater choice. The candidate can choose the date as well as the venue of the Interview. There are four Air Force Selection Boards operation located at Dehradun in Uttarakhand, Mysore in Karnataka, Varanasi in Uttar Pradesh and Gandhinagar in Gujarat.

It is necessary that logistical aspects are taken in consideration while selecting the venue and date as in most of the cases a change in date is not allowed. It is recommended that the date selected is not of the last few batches as there will be a greater number of candidates appearing for them. Do take into consideration the level of physical fitness and medical fitness before choosing the date.

CHAPTER THREE

Documentation for the SSB Interview

What truly defines an officer is the level of order and discipline maintained throughout. Documentation is an important part of this. After selecting the date for the SSB Interview, the candidate receives a Call Letter with detailed instructions. This has to be read and adhered to the last letter as they do not expect anything other than that mentioned in the Call Letter. It is necessary that the following documents are always ready and arranged in an order as mentioned in the Call Letter.

1. Online Application
2. Call Letter
3. Admit Card
4. Original Identity Proof
5. 10th Mark sheet and Certificate
6. 12th Mark sheet and Certificate
7. Degree Certificate for all entries other than NDA and TES
8. Graduation Mark sheets for all entries other than NDA and TES

9. Bonafide Certificate if studying in Final year of graduation
10. Declaration of marks if applying on the basis of graduation
11. National Cadet Corps (NCC) C Certificate if applying for NCC entry
12. Any other document as mentioned in the Call Letter or website instructions

It is obligatory that all the documents have to be in original with at least two sets of photo copies self attested. It is good if one more set of un-attested photo copies is carried. This would be helpful if additional copies are required where one can avoid taking out originals and the photocopies themselves.

The documents shall be arranged neatly in a folder file for easy presentation. The Call Letter instructions mention certain documents to be shown at the reporting point and some other for the initial documentation. Care needs to be taken that all the mentioned documents are in the correct order and handy. Photocopies may be kept in a separate folder but try to maintain only one folder throughout the process.

CHAPTER FOUR

Traveling from home for the SSB Interview

Now that you have all the documents ready for the interview according to the call letter, it's time to plan for the journey. It is always advisable that the candidate reaches the city where the interview is being conducted at least a day in advance to settle down and stay fresh for the process.

At first, I would like to tell about some journey hacks and things to remember for different modes of transport and thereafter a few important words of caution out of experience.

Lesser luggage equals more comfort. This should be mantra while packing the luggage for the interview. Out of my experience, one bag is sufficient to carry the required luggage for a period of at least 10 days provided it is packed smartly. The Call letter contains details of all the necessary items to be carried. Candidates are encouraged to avoid taking unnecessary items like iron box and so on as at most of the boards, there is a facility available on payment.

The journey should be comfortable and cost effective. During my attempts, I have used all the three modes of transport viz. air, rail and road out of which railway is the most comfortable and pocket friendly at the same time. However, there may be constraints of time which may call for alternate modes of transport which may be chosen at discretion. This is where, that one bag makes the journey comfortable by avoiding any kind of additional attention to be given to multiple bags.

Air Travel is comparatively the most expensive yet the fastest mode of transport. This would be recommended to those who are working and have issues with regards to leaves. As most of the cities that have selection boards of the three services are well connected by air, the candidate can easily reach the city. However, there are a few cities whose airports are located quite far away like Bangalore where it would take an equivalent time to reach the selection centre from the airport. It is advisable that the candidates carry a small backpack as a cabin luggage so that certain items like power banks which are not allowed in the check in luggage can be kept with oneself. During air travel, you can definitely enjoy the scenic beauty of the landscapes and feel motivated indeed. The gushing of adrenaline when the aircraft is running up for the take off is an experience beyond words. The Boarding Pass has to be kept safe if the candidate is claiming the traveling allowance.

Indian Railways never fail to make every journey memorable if you are planning to use this mode of transport. I can write volumes together on all my experiences with Indian railways. For candidates traveling for SSB Interview, I feel the Side Upper Berth in any class would be the ideal one owing to its combination of personal space and vacancy throughout the day. One can sleep through the day and relax without being disturbed. While traveling by train, make sure the luggage is under lock and key and is chained to the clamps. This keeps the mind at peace! During the early hours of the mornings or during sunsets, one can witness the beauty of the landscape of our country at different parts. Things to eat and people to talk around add a flavor to the journey which would otherwise be quite mundane. As a few service selection boards call the candidates to report at the railway station of the city, this mode of transport is best one to save on time. Indian Railways has excellent retiring rooms which can be booked well in advance and the facilities can be beautifully availed.

Road transport choice depends on the traveler. Some may prefer Bus while some may prefer private vehicles. However, if the travel time is beyond 12 hours, road transport should be avoided to avoid fatigue and motion sickness.

On reaching the city, it is necessary to lodge at a decent place to have proper rest so that you are ready for testing.

There is a well plot scam that I would like to bring to the notice of all the aspirants. This generally happens with those who arrive by train but may start at the airport as well. One would agree that after a long time of traveling, the candidate is quite tired and is in search of an easy way to find a hotel to lodge. Some candidates who travel alone do not carry out an initial study or survey of nearby hotels which leads to them getting trapped in the scam.

It starts at the railways station where an auto rickshaw driver identifies the potential bait by recognizing the haircut and paraphernalia. He addresses as 'Sir' and the 'Sir' is happy to get this treatment. The moment you start walking with him, you are into the scam and it is impossible to get out of it now. After promising that he would come the next morning right on time to drop you to the SSB, he takes you to a nearby hotel. The scam is that the hotel tells wrong tariff and demands a greater tariff the next day morning when you are in a hurry to report at the SSB. The auto driver gets a sumptuous commission and may not even turn up the next morning. Thus it is necessary to be vigilant and avoid falling prey to such traps.

CHAPTER FIVE

Reporting for the SSB Interview

The Call Letter contains clear information regarding the date, time and location of reporting. The date is as chosen by you after the announcement of results. The time of reporting depends on the board but the same is generally 0630 hrs or earlier is the Screening is going to be conducted on the same day. The time of reporting may be 1400 hrs one day prior to the start of the selection procedure if the Board conducts documentation a day in advance and starts with the screening tests on the next day.

There are a few boards where the reporting has to be done at the railway station while at others it is directly at the board itself. It is the responsibility of the candidate to ensure that he/she is on time at the reporting point.

If traveling by air, make sure the travel time from the airport to the reporting point is adequate enough to be on time. Late running trains also need to be considered if traveling by train. It is good to reach the reporting point certain time in advance so that one can get acquainted with a few fellow candidates. Remember that SSB is not a competition but a personality test where it is necessary to build a good bond with the fellow candidates. A brief talk can be an effective way to get gelled up. Most of the times, the first question asked at the reporting point by fellow candidates is whether you are a fresher or repeater and then the conversation continues. There is a secret of recognizing freshers. Most of them may have their parents or guardians accompanying them and it is a mandatory ritual for most of the freshers to carry a newspaper. To be honest, I too had bought The Times of India at Bangalore Railway station when I was a fresher.

If the reporting is at the railway station, try to locate the Movement Control Office (MCO) in advance and report at the location on time. A bus will come to pick you up at that time. Certain documents like call letter and original identity proof should be kept handy for an initial verification. If reporting directly at the board, reach at least half an hour in advance so that there is no last minute rush. Once you are in, rest is taken care of by the personnel at the board.

CHAPTER SIX

What not to do on Day 1: Documentation and Screening Tests

There are certain boards that may conduct the documentation a day prior to the screening tests while most of them conduct the documentation on the same day as that of the screening tests or what is commonly called as Stage 1 Testing.

6.1 Documentation at the Services Selection Board

Once the candidates enter the premises of the Services Selection Board, they are made to place their luggage in a designated area. In all probability this area is under CCTV surveillance hence there is nobody who can dare steal anything but it is always advisable that everything is kept under lock and key.

Thereafter there are certain basic instructions given to the candidates regarding conduct and the documents required for a preliminary document check. These documents mostly include the Online Application, Admit Card, Call Letter, academic records and identity proofs. It is better to keep these documents handy. The order in which the candidates may be called varies from board to board. Some boards may consider fresher or repeater basis, some the age and so on.

To avoid any kind of routing back due to non availability of documents, it is better to read the call up instructions and keep all the documents ready as mentioned in the formats and annexure provided.

Once the document verification is completed, the candidates may be sent for breakfast. At times the breakfast may take place after the chest numbers are allotted. Chest numbers are allotted according to the board's discretion. Some boards may start from repeaters while some from freshers. At some boards, age may be considered while at some it may be on first come first serve basis.

Please remember:

- Don't keep your luggage scattered. Keep everything together
- Don't keep any bags open.
- Lock all your belongings especially those having food items as there is every chance that rodents like squirrels can relish on them
- Never override the instructions with regards to behaviour and conduct
- Don't miss any document and follow the sequence as told during the briefing

6.2 Officer Intelligence Rating (OIR) Tests

This is first of the two tests conducted for Stage 1 testing. The purpose of this test is to ascertain the level of intelligence of the candidate. It needs to be noted that no tests or tasks at the services selection board interview are competitive in nature as they assess individual psychological traits which vary from person to person.

The candidates are made to sit in the testing hall and the duty selection officer may give an opening address followed by certain instructions to be followed during the stay. Once the candidates have settled down, the test booklets are provided. These test booklets are a property of Defence Institute of Psychological Research (DIPR) and are completely confidential. Thus it is necessary that none of the questions are recorded or reproduced outside in any manner. The booklets have been provided with different numbered series like 34, 35, 52, 53, 71, 72 and so on. Having appeared for the screening test 22 times, I have even seen some other series than those mentioned here and at times there have been repetitions is different interviews as well. Thus it is likely that if a candidate is a repeater, he/she must have answered that particular series somewhere else earlier. However, this does not add any advantage because the tests and tasks are designed in such a manner that freshers and repeaters are at the same advantage and disadvantage. It is the performance that matters.

At first, an illustration and practice booklet is provided. Make sure you understand each and every question as the test booklets shall have questions similar to the ones mentioned in the illustration and practice set. I have realized that to excel in SSB, one must adhere to the instructions in totality. The instructions are in a way hints to perform better in the tasks. Solve the practice set with concentration to build confidence.

Most of the tests at the SSB are based on the concept of time stress where the time is less and the amount of work seems to be large. This according to research brings out the true personality of the candidate in which there cannot be any kind of bluffing. The officer intelligence tests are designed in such a way that the candidate's ability to solve problems correctly and quickly is assessed. The problems may be of verbal or non verbal type. Some series contain problems which involve calculations. Some logical reasoning problems are based on pictorial series and some on analogies, coding and decoding. As per my experience, no special preparation is required and the candidate can easily answer the questions if the illustration and practice set is properly understood.

Please remember:

- Don't override any of the instructions
- Don't indulge in malpractices like copying or marking the booklets in any manner as the chest number may be noted and the candidate may be penalized
- Don't record or reproduce any of the questions from the test booklets outside in any form
- Don't make any mistakes while marking the answer sheets
- Don't forget to encircle the series of the booklet received by you for the test
- Don't sit thinking about the difficult questions. Proceed to the next one

- There is no negative marking. So at the end, for those questions that were left blank, it would be advisable to mark the most probable answer according to you
- Start when you are told to start and stop when you are told to do so

6.3 Picture Perception and Discussion Test (PPDT)

This is the second test conducted for Stage 1 testing. This test is divided into two parts viz. the picture perception test and second is the discussion test. The candidates are divided into smaller groups of say 50 to 60 and are taken to the testing hall. After seating the candidates, a psychologist or the Technical Officer may come to brief about the test. Listen carefully to the briefing as the assessor is then telling you how to do well in the test. After the briefing is done the conducted as follows.

The candidates are shown a hazy picture for 30 seconds. During this time, it is required that the candidate observes the picture carefully and makes a mental note of the number of characters, their sex, age and mood and the current situation in the picture. Thereafter 1 minute is given to mark these details on the answer sheet in a square box. It is noteworthy that one of the characters has to be encircled. This is the character first seen by you in the picture. It has been a wrong notion that story should revolve around this central character. It is not so. Your story is your perception. After marking the details, the candidate has to write the action which indicates what is currently happening as perceived in the picture. Thereafter 4 minutes are given to write the story. It is required that the story revolves around the characters perceived by you. It is necessary to mention what led to the situation, what is going on and what is the likely outcome. While writing this, the candidate is expected to write the feelings, thoughts and emotions of the characters without any regards for beauty of expression. It is recommended that the language used is English but if stuck somewhere, Hindi words can be used but do revert back to English as soon as possible. The story should be written in a minimum of 100 words which can be easily written within 4 minutes with a legible handwriting. It may be noted that although there are no extra marks for good handwriting, a legible and neat writing can tell a lot about the personality of the candidate. Once the time is up, the assessor will indicate the same wherein the candidate shall stop writing and put their pen down. This fairly completes the first part of the picture perception and discussion test. After this, the candidates are taken out and are divided into smaller groups for the next test which is the discussion test.

For the discussion test, the size of the group may be anywhere between 10 to 30 depending on the logistical aspects at the board like the number of discussion rooms and panels available. It is necessary to note that number of candidates in a group does not have any connection with the number of candidates chosen from that group. It is purely based on performance. The candidates are then taken to a designated Discussion Room where the assessors are present. It is generally 3 assessors and any additional assessor is a trainee. The panel of assessors contains a Psychologist, a Group Task Officer (GTO) and an Interviewing Officer. All of them are in civil dress to avoid any kind of fear or excitement due to uniform. Once the candidates have seated, the GTO starts with the briefing for the next task. The discussion is carried out in continuation to the picture perception test. The candidates may be provided with the sheets on which they had written the stories and could be given a chance to revise the same in half a minute. Every candidate is generally provided one minute to narrate the individual story in which it is expected that the narration is short and crisp. If the assessors get the central idea or if the candidates are overshooting the time limit, they may be asked to stop and the next candidate shall start with their narration immediately. Once the last candidate has completed their narration, it is expected that the group spontaneously starts with the discussion. It is natural that in the first few minutes, as everyone tries to speak, there may be some noise but it is a skill to find that moment of silence where you can start putting your point. Don't be a bully instead try to intervene and try to get a common consensus because the aim of the discussion is not to decide whose story was the best but to arrive at a common consensus which is a story that most of them if not all of them would agree upon. It may also be noted that there is no special marking for the candidate who initiates or concludes the discussion.

After the discussion test is completed, the candidates are marched to the Mess where a sumptuous meal is awaiting to be tasted by the candidates. Certain basic Mess etiquettes are expected from the candidates but it is nowhere concerned with the candidate's performance in the interview.

Please remember the following for the picture perception test:

- Don't overlook any of the points mentioned in the briefing as the assessor is indirectly telling you how to excel in the test
- Don't start marking the answer sheet when the picture is being displayed. Observe the picture carefully and make a mental note of the details required to be marked
- Don't waste too much of time in decorating the square box. Complete it with the action statement under a minute and start writing the story
- Don't write a too short story. It should be at least 100 words. At the same time, ensure that you don't write too long a story to get confused later
- Don't write in an illegible handwriting as presentation of thoughts does matter during evaluation
- There is nothing like central character. You have to encircle the details of the first character seen by you in the picture
- Don't try to link every story to defence or similar genres as it can be made out. Instead write a realistic story. Something similar to the picture that must have happened in your life would be a great idea as you can be highly expressive and truthful
- Don't complicate the story to get confused later. Keep it simple
- Don't use any language other than English or Hindi as per instructions given
- Don't continue to write after the time is up
- Don't discuss your story with anybody before the discussion test

Please remember the following for the discussion test:

- Don't get overwhelmed by the number of candidates in your group as it is mostly a logistical concern and your performance is carefully evaluated for selection
- Don't be nervous. All the group members are of your age group and of similar experience
- During the narration, don't exceed the time limit of 1 minute given by the Group Task Officer
- Don't feel shy to initiate the discussion. Take the plunge!
- Don't try to suppress anybody's ideas as it gives a wrong impression. Intervene instead and find common grounds. This displays good management of ideas
- Try to be with the group and don't advertize your own story
- If nominated by the group to narrate the common consensus, don't repeat your own story but try to make a common story which is a result of the group discussion
- Don't be gloomy or pessimistic. Wear a smile but don't laugh out loud!
- Maintain an upright disciplined posture and never lose the calm

The results for Stage 1 Testing are announced right after the lunch. This may get delayed at times if the number of candidates is large. But with most probability, results of screening are announced by 1400 hrs.

For the results, the candidates are taken to the testing hall or a designated location. The chest numbers of successful candidates are called out while those who cannot make it are dropped back at the Railway Station.

Those who have been selected for Stage 2 testing spanning over the next three days with the Board Conference on the last day are asked to relocate their luggage to another designated area. This is followed by a detailed round of documentation.

All the documents brought by the candidate are verified and deposited. The most important document to be filled in by the candidate is the Personal Information Questionnaire (PIQ) Form. A candidate has to fill up two copies of the same out of which one is the basis for the personal interview and the other is referred by the psychologist. The format and instructions to fill will be told accordingly. It is required that all the information written therein shall be true and not bluffed or concealed. This is especially required with respect the number and details of the previous attempts at the SSB. Don't hide any information as according to my observation, all the attempts are digitally saved and one can at least see the history of the same on the website of joinindianarmy.

After the documentation is done, the time would be around 1700 hrs and the candidates are allotted their rooms and beds. Generally at the Air Force Selection Boards, the Psychological Tests are conducted on the same day in the evening after 1800 hrs and run up to 2230 hrs hence the candidates are required to be ready for a long day of testing. Detailed schedule of testing is adequately briefed by the duty selection officers accordingly. In this book, the most generally followed schedule has been considered. At other boards, the evenings are generally free and the candidates can use this time to build a good bond among them. Games like table tennis or carrom may be played.

It is advisable that the candidate sleeps on time so that he/she is ready and fresh for the Psychological Tests next day.

CHAPTER SEVEN

What not to do on Day 2: Psychological Tests and Personal Interview

7.1 Psychological Tests

In this technique, intellect of the candidate is assessed. This is the only technique where the assessor does not meet the candidate in person but tries to build a personality based on the responses given to a wide range of stimuli. It is noteworthy that all these tests are under time stress and the candidate is likely to display their true personality through their responses. There are four tests which have been elaborated as follows.

7.1.1 Thematic Apperception Test (TAT)

In this test, the candidates are shown a total of 11 pictures and 1 blank slide and they are expected to write a story in a manner similar to that followed during the picture perception test with the only variation being that in TAT, the marking of characters and action is not required to be written.

The candidates are provided with booklets where around half a page space is available to write the story. With the advent of technology, the tests are now administered by software that accurately keeps the time. The procedure is quite simple. The candidates are shown a picture for 30 seconds and then 4 minutes are given to write the story. This is repeated for 11 slides with pictures and the last slide is a blank slide.

When the blank slide is being displayed, instead of rushing to write a prepared story, just keep gazing at the blank screen. You may come up with a new story which may be similar to some of them written earlier. It would be highly recommended that such spontaneous story is written as the 12th one.

After this test is completed, the Word Association Test is conducted.

Please remember:

- Don't fall short or exceed the word limit as told by the psychologist
- Observation of the picture should be done carefully. Don't start writing when the picture is being shown
- Try to make a story in your mind simultaneously as you are observing
- All the stories need not be purposely knitted to each other. They may be diametrically opposite if so perceived by you
- Don't prepare a story for the Blank Slide at the end. Instead write something spontaneously. It will depict

your true personality
- Don't let your handwriting get shabby by the end as presentation is necessarily important
- Your perception is correct according to you. Don't discuss your stories with anybody

7.1.2 Word Association Test (WAT)

In this test, the ability to express ideas on stimulus is tested. This test is also administered by the software. In this a word is displayed on the screen for 15 seconds within which, the candidate has to see the word and write a sentence associated with it. 60 such words are shown and the total time taken is 15 minutes.

It may happen at times that the same word is repeated or a similar word is repeated. It is advisable that the candidate does not waste time in searching for the previous answer. Spontaneous responses are always in favour of the candidate.

A word displayed may be perceived differently by different candidates according to their intellectual thought process. Thus there is no right and wrong as far as writing sentences based on displayed words is concerned.

Please remember:

- Don't write phrases or idioms having the word displayed
- Keep track of the word number as most of the times only the word is displayed and there is no number beside it
- Try to write complete meaningful sentences
- There is nothing like negative or positive words. It all depends on your perception

7.1.3 Situation Reaction Test (SRT)

This is the third test in the psychological tests technique. This is not administered by software and is conducted using booklets. There are 60 situation questions that have to be answered in 30 minutes. The candidate can take any amount of time to address a particular question but it is expected that maximum answers are provided so that the assessment can be done accordingly.

In the booklet, there is every probability that similar situations may be posed at different question numbers. This tests your true personality through the responses. It is good if realistic responses are given and faking any kind of adventure is avoided.

Please remember:

- Don't include armed forces related answers in all situations
- Read the situation completely and not only the keywords
- Don't try to write vague answers or actions that you would never do as the other tests speak volumes about your personality
- Don't write in phrases but write your response in full sentences
- Be practical and provide proper solutions and actions to the situations

7.1.4 Self Description Test (SDT)

This is the only test whose responses can be prepared in advance. However, any additional instructions given at the time of test need to be adhered to. The psychologist provides instructions as to the way in which the responses have to be written. In this test, 5 different paragraphs have to be written in 15 minutes. In these paragraphs, opinions of various near and dear ones has to be penned down frankly.

1. The first paragraph is about opinion of your parents or guardians about you. It is natural that parents would consider their children to be excellent but in case parents have been suggesting improvements or correcting at times, it must reflect in their opinion as well.
2. The second paragraph is about the opinion of your teachers (if studying) or employer (if working) about you. These opinions can be understood during the parent teacher meetings or during appraisals at office.
3. The third paragraph is about the opinion of friends or colleagues about you. These may be understood by having healthy discussions with the interested parties. However it is good if the honest opinions are included.
4. The fourth paragraph is about the self image. We at times have superiority or inferiority complexes. These may be projected by the psychologist through earlier responses and this paragraph would just be a confirmation of the same.
5. The fifth and last paragraph is about the kind of person you would like to become. None of us are completely perfect and there is always a room for improvement and ambitions. In this paragraph, all such ambitions need to be depicted honestly

Please remember:

- Don't lie any of the opinions
- Responses can be based on discussions done earlier
- Faking a personality would not match with the responses given in the earlier tests

With this test, the Psychological tests are completed and the detailed evaluation is commenced. The candidate is thereafter subjected to two more techniques viz. the Interviewing technique and Group Tasks technique.

7.2 Personal Interview

In this technique, the expression of the candidate is assessed. Compared to the other two techniques, this technique takes lesser time but is equally capable of deciding the chances of recommendation of the candidate.

The personal interview may be conducted on any of the days before the Board Conference depending on the schedule planned by the board. It is generally the Board President or the Deputy President who interviews the candidate. The candidate is informed about the time of their Interview well in advance so that adequate time is available to dress up. However, the candidate can be interviewed in the GTO dress itself if so required.

In the armed forces, there is importance given to reporting at the right place at the right time in the right rig i.e. dress. Thus it is imperative for the candidate to adhere to the instructions given. Just before the interview, the candidate is taken to a waiting room where they can find certain magazines or a television. There is no need to get overwhelmed by these and self confidence is the key.

In a few boards, the candidates are required to carry their certificates along with them while in a few boards photocopies are placed on the interviewer's table. There will be most probably only one Interviewing Officer but in case there are more, the candidate may assume that they are trainees.

Once the Interviewing Officer calls the candidate, it is required that the candidate enters, greets the officer and sits when told to be seated. It completely depends on the process as to how long would the interview last. It may take anywhere between 15 minutes to 2 hours.

During the interview, the officer generally starts with a series of questions which may be related to academics, family, job and so on. It is necessary to remember the sequence of the questions and answer them in the same sequence. It is not that in all the interviews, rapid fire questions are asked. Similar is the case with questions on general knowledge. It completely depends on the interviewing officer.

Freshers are generally asked with a few ice breakers since they are going through the process first time. There may be a few questions like favourite movies and actors to calm them from the anxiety and bring the best out of them.

Repeaters are generally asked questions related to performance improvements compared to the previous attempts. It is expected that they must have worked on their weaker areas and developed their personality accordingly.

The information provided in the Personal Information Questionnaire (PIQ) form is the basis for the interview. At times certain questions may be extrapolated or interpolated to establish the personality of the candidate. It is natural to be nervous and anxious during the interview even for repeaters. However, good amount of self confidence can work out wonders.

Please remember:

- Don't dress inappropriately. Look like a gentleman since you are addressed as one
- Don't offer your hand unless the officer offers it to you
- Sit only when you are asked to do so
- Don't murmur. It is good to be loud and clear but at the same time it is not advised to shout
- Don't look serious. Smile is a good way to relieve tension
- Don't hesitate to drink water from the glass kept beside you
- Don't be in a hurry to answer the questions. Take your time and answer to the point
- Don't even think of bluffing or lying as it is easily caught by your own answer to some other question. Be yourself
- Don't mess up answers. Be clear in your comprehension

CHAPTER EIGHT

What not to do on Day 3: Group Tasks Day 1

In this technique, the candidate's ability to execute tasks is assessed. While the psychological tests and the interview are individual tasks, the group tasks are done in a group except the lecturette and the individual obstacles.

The basis of this technique is the time stress and resource stress under which the candidates have to work as a group and execute a given task with the available helping material. The group tasks are conducted over a span of two days to ensure physical stamina and open mindedness of the candidates.

On the days of group tasks, the candidates are expected to wake up earlier than others and report to the designated point by 0630 hrs. The candidates are divided into smaller groups of six to ten candidates each for the next two days of group tasks. Every group is assigned with a Group Testing Officer who will be their assessor.

It is necessary to note that a test has a fixed solution while a task does not have a fixed solution. Thus there is no right or wrong process if the objective is achieved.

8.1 Group Discussion (GD) (2 rounds)

There are two rounds of Group discussion each lasting around 20 minutes. In the first round, the candidates are required to choose among two topics given by the GTO and then discuss on the same. In the second round, the GTO will be giving a topic to discuss and the group has to abide by it.

The initial briefing says that the discussion shall be something like that seen in a college canteen or a casual meet up. But there are many candidates who mistake it to be a debate and this is what ruins the fun. It is an activity wherein mutual understanding can be built, each others opinions on various topics can be comprehended and so on. There may be a few candidates in favour of the topic while a few against. The aim should be to put forward points and not to arrive at any kind of consensus.

Please remember:

- Don't consider this as a debate. It should sound like a healthy discussion
- Don't throw absurd points. It is advisable to provide facts and figures
- Don't simply agree with a candidate to display presence. Contribute a valid point instead
- Don't yell at any candidate if the point put forward by them is not in agreement with your thought process

The aim of this task is to initiate a feeling of expression among the candidates and a bond of mutual trust for the further tasks

8.2 Group Planning Exercise (GPE)

This task evaluates the ability to solve multiple problems as a group. In most of the Service Selection Boards, there are painted Boards that are displayed as models while at a few Air Force Selection Boards, there are three dimensional models. The models are provided with minute details with name tags and so on.

There is a narrative which is initially read out by the GTO. The narrative presents a situation where as a group, the candidates are going for some work, say to attend a function at their college. On their way, they come across three to four problems of different levels of severity. There are certain constraints on time and resources and modes of transport. The narrative describes all the problems and towards the end asks the group to provide the best feasible solution to the same.

It is necessary that the candidates observe the model carefully when the GTO is reading out the narrative and pointing out towards the various highlights and features. Thereafter the candidates are handed over the narrative sheets and they are expected to read the same and make a mental plan. Thereafter the candidates are given 10 minutes to write their action plan to solve the problems. Once the individual solutions are written, the group is expected to discuss and arrive at a common consensus of solution of the problems.

Among the problems stated, one affects a large population and is of high importance, other two can be solved alternately and one is the least important which can be solved with lesser attention. Thus it is required that within the stipulated time, the candidates are able to find a solution such that all the problems are addressed and they are able to move to their actual task of attending the function at their college.

Please remember:

- Don't get distracted while the GTO is briefing
- Don't overlook minor details like the distances and accessibility displayed on the model or board
- Don't jump to conclusions. Prioritization is a must
- Don't forget to solve the minor problems
- Don't miss to add completion of the basic task that the group wanted to do like they were going to attend a function and they attended it in time after settling the situation

8.3 Progressive Group Task (PGT)

This is the first on field task in the GTO series. In this task, the group is expected to cross four obstacles one after the other which progressively gets difficult. There is a certain helping material given to the candidates and a few basic rules are to be followed.

The task begins with a briefing explaining all the obstacles, rules, colour codes and so on. It is necessary to stay attentive during the briefing as the GTO is indirectly telling how the tasks have to be done successfully. The time within which the task has to be completed shall be briefed by the GTO although any kinds of time keeping devices are not allowed or available for reference.

The candidates need to make the best use of the helping material and abiding by the rules have to cross the obstacles. There is generally a heavy box that symbolizes a casualty which has to be taken along with the group. At times, the GTO may change a few rules on the spot just to test the ability to work under pressure.

Please remember:

- Try to suggest solutions and not impose them
- Don't try to ridicule the solutions of any candidate
- Don't break any of the rules related to colour, infinity or helping material
- Take the group together
- Don't forget to make a plan as to how would the last man cross the obstacle
- Don't damage any of the helping material intentionally
- Don't get stressed out when the GTO starts warning about the time. It is done at times to induce more time stress

8.4 Group Obstacle Race (GOR) or Snake Race

This task is conducted to instill some josh in the candidates. All the groups compete against each other and negotiate six different obstacles simultaneously. While doing so, they have to carry a long bag filled with sand which is also called as a snake. Hence the name snake race. The rules for the task shall be briefed by the senior GTO and the same have to be adhered to.

The first obstacle is a simple ramp jump while the second is the task of forming the digit 8 between three horizontal bars. In the third obstacle, the candidates have to cross a spider web like structure.

The fourth obstacle is a double wall in which the first wall has to be climbed up and the one has to cross to the second via a bar and then jump to the ground. The fifth obstacle is a single wall which is comparatively higher than the double wall which has to be climbed and jumped from. The sixth obstacle is a combination of a slitted ramp and a slide on the other side.

For breaking any of the rules, there may be a penalty imposed to the effect of repeating an obstacle a certain number of times.

Please remember:

- Don't hold the snake on one side only. Holding it on alternate sides of candidates would be much better
- Make sure while negotiating the obstacles, at least three candidates are holding the snake
- Don't leave the snake while running between the obstacles
- Ask for help if there is any problem in negotiating an obstacle
- Avoid wearing canvas shoes as they do not provide necessary grip. Use sports shoes of white colour
- In event of any kind of giddiness, ask for help from the groundsmen immediately

8.5 Half Group Task (HGT)

This task is completely similar to the Progressive Group Task with a minor variation being that the number of candidates is exactly half of the original number in the group. It is a task to check the ability to cross obstacles with half the number of group members i.e. with limited resources.

8.6 Lecturette

Lecturette is the last task on the first day of GTO. In this task, the candidate is given three topics to choose one for a lecture of around 3 minutes. This task tries to evaluate public speaking skills of the candidate. The traits of confidence and courage to face the group are required to complete this task.

Please remember:

- Don't choose a topic that you are unsure about as it may land you to confusion
- There is no problem if you fumble. Correct yourself and continue
- Try to give facts and examples

CHAPTER NINE

What not to do on Day 4: Group Tasks Day 2

9.1 Individual Obstacles (IO)

This is the first task on the second day of GTO testing. There are a series of 10 obstacles that have been numbered serially and bear the same number of marks if completed according to the rules. There are a few obstacles that are optional for the female candidates which will be briefed accordingly.

The obstacles are enlisted as follows:

1. Single Ramp
2. Double Barrel
3. Balancing Beam
4. Screen Jump
5. Burma Bridge
6. Tarzan Jump
7. Double Jump
8. Double Ditch

9. Commando Walk
10. Tiger Leap

Please remember:

- Ensure you are warmed up before you start with the obstacles
- Don't jump with locked knees as it can lead to stress fracture
- Handle the rope carefully and avoid any palm burns
- Don't wear canvas shoes as they are likely to slip. Use sports shoes
- Don't touch any surface painted red as it is out of bounds
- Don't get down from the Balance Beam in between else it has to be repeated
- Don't repeat an obstacle unless one complete cycle is done
- Hold the rope tight in Tarzan Jump
- Clasp the rope tightly in Tiger Leap
- Have high levels of confidence and a feeling that you can do it!

9.2 Command Task (CT)

In this task, every candidate is made the commander of a squad of 2 other sub ordinates that can be chosen from the group. The GTO calls the candidates and conducts a brief discussion asking various aspects of the stay and places visited if any during their stay at the SSB. The task to be done is generally decided based on the candidate's ability as evaluated by the GTO.

After a brief discussion, the GTO explains the task to the commander and two sub ordinates are selected. The commander is required to demonstrate and complete the task as asked by the GTO. The GTO may add further constraints to confirm the candidate's abilities to a further extent.

Please remember:

- Try to follow 'Do and demonstrate' concept in which you as a leader show the execution of the task
- Commander leads from front
- Don't ask for suggestions unless ultimately necessary
- Ensure the squad selected is capable of completing the task

9.3 Final Group Task (FGT)

This task is similar to the Progressive group task with minor changes in the obstacles and is used as a confirmation of the candidate's performance.

There is a debriefing done after the task where the GTO may have an informal discussion with the candidates. Further procedure of conference may be told in short and certain tips for career may also be shared.

CHAPTER TEN

What not to do on Day 5: The Board Conference

The Board Conference is a highly formal occasion where all the assessors come together and discuss the performance of the candidate and make a decision about the recommendation. Prior to the Conference, the Board President delivers a motivational talk to the candidates.

Please remember:

- Enter the Conference Room with confidence, greet the President and sit when you are asked to do so
- Don't dress in clumsy attire. It is always good to be simple yet properly turned out
- Never button your shirt's top most button unless you are wearing a tie
- Don't roll up sleeves of your shirt
- Answer confidently
- Don't hesitate to give your valuable suggestions for improvement
- Leave the room after thanking the President

With this, the services selection board interview is concluded and the candidates are marched to the Mess for lunch. In a manner similar to the results of Stage 1, the results of Stage 2 are announced and the recommended candidates are retained for the medicals. I am not eligible to write anything about the medicals as I have never undergone them. Those candidates who are not recommended are dropped at the railway station or are free to take their own transport.

CHAPTER ELEVEN

Traveling back home from the SSB Interview

Whether screened out, not recommended or recommended, it is necessary to have solid plan for each situation before leaving home. If the SSB City is located far away, it is always good to keep back up plans ready at dispense.

For Air travel, booking needs to be done at least four hours in advance to avoid escalated costs while for trains, if possible Tatkal tickets can be booked. In my opinion, it is not advisable to pre book return tickets looking at the uncertainty of selection.

If not selected this time, try harder the next time!

Remember that,

> *"*"At times, failures need to be swallowed so that success can be sumptuously relished and digested one day!"*"*

All the Best!!

www.ingramcontent.com/pod-product-compliance
Lightning Source LLC
LaVergne TN
LVHW021737060526
838200LV00052B/3322